WE LAUGH

Riddles and Jokes

for Kids 9-12

Riddles for kids

Many of us can agree: the triumph that comes with solving a tough riddle is a feeling like no other.

And chances are, your child will love riddles too!

Riddles aren't only fun, but they can help boost your children's verbal fluency, problem-solving skills, and creative thinking. Riddles, and other brain teaser-type verbal puzzles, typically rely on clever new angles to look at something common, or on words with veiled or multiple meanings.

Riddle 1

What has to be broken before you can use it?

Answer

An egg.

Riddle 2

The more you take, the more you leave behind.

What am I?

Answer

Footsteps

Riddle 3

If two's company, and three's a crowd,
what are four and five?

Answer

Nine!

Riddle 4

After a train crashed, every single person died.

Who survived?

Answer

All of the couples.

Riddle 5

A boy and his father get into a car accident. When they arrive at the hospital, the doctor sees the boy and exclaims "That's my son!" How can this be?

Answer

The doctor is the boy's mother.

Riddle 6

Four legs up, four legs down,
soft in the middle,
Hard all around.

Answer

Bed

Riddle 7

What can you catch but not throw?

Answer
A cold!

Riddle 8

What begins with T, finishes with T, and has T in it?

Answer

A teapot.

Riddle 9

If a brother, his sister, and their dog weren't under an umbrella, why didn't they get wet?

Answer

It wasn't raining

Riddle 10

I am so simple,
that I can only point
yet I guide men all over the world

Answer

Compass

Riddle 11

What goes up but never comes back down?

Answer

Your Age

Riddle 12

What five-letter word becomes shorter when you add two letters to it?

Answer

Shorter. (Short + 'er')

Riddle 13

What travels around the world but stays in one spot?

Answer

A stamp.

Riddle 14

When things go wrong,
what can you always count on?

Answer

Your fingers.

Riddle 15

Mr. Blue lives in the Blue house.

Mrs. Yellow lives in the Yellow House.

Mr. Orange lives in the orange house.

Who lives in the White House?

Answer

The President

Riddle 16

A word I know, six letters it contains remove one letter and 12 remains, what is it?

Answer

Dozen

Riddle 17

What is full of holes but still holds water?

Answer

Sponge

Riddle 18

How many letters are there in the English alphabet?

Answer

18: 3 in 'the', 7 in 'English,' and 8 in 'alphabet.'

Riddle 19

If a red house is made of red bricks, and a yellow house is made of yellow bricks, what is a greenhouse made of?

Answer

Glass, all greenhouses are made of glass.

Riddle 20

What begins with an E but only has one letter?

Answer

An envelope.

Riddle 21

You draw a line. Without touching it, how do you make it a longer line?

Answer

Draw a short line next to it and now it's the longer line.

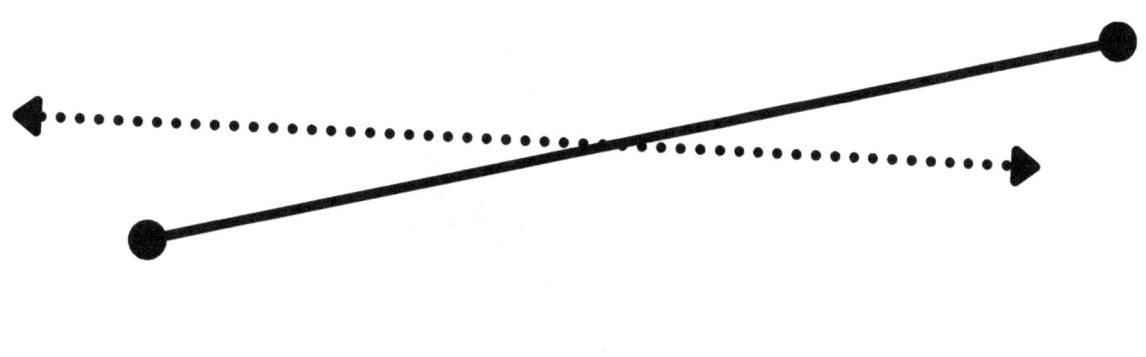

Riddle 22

How can a leopard change its spots?

Answer

By moving from one spot to another.

Riddle 23

What is easy to get into but hard to get out of?

Answer

Trouble.

Riddle 24

Mary has four daughters,
and each of her daughters has a brother
— how many children does Mary have?

Answer

Five, each daughter has the same brother.

Riddle 25

David's parents have three sons: Snap, Crackle and...?

Answer

David!

Riddle 26

You bought me for dinner but never eat me.
What am I?

Answer

Cutlery

Riddle 27

I'm tall when I'm young, and I'm short when I'm old, what am I?

Answer

A candle.

Riddle 28

What answer can you never answer yes to?

Answer

Are you asleep yet?

Riddle 29

What is so fragile that saying its name breaks it?

Answer

Silence.

Riddle 30

I am an odd number. Take away a letter and I become even. What number am I?

Answer

Seven.

Riddle 31

What has a head, a tail, is brown, and has no legs?

Answer

A penny.

Riddle 32

What is always in front of you but can't be seen?

Answer

The future.

Riddle 33

What's black and white and blue?

Answer

A sad zebra.

Riddle 34

What has four eyes but can't see?

Answer

Mississippi.

Riddle 35

Where can you find cities, towns, shops, and streets but no people?

Answer

A map

Riddle 36

What has a neck but no head?

Answer

Bottle

Riddle 37

What word is spelled wrong in the dictionary?

Answer

Wrong.

Riddle 38

If you took two apples from a pile
of three apples,
how many apples would you have?

Answer

The one apple you took

Riddle 39

Light as a feather, there's nothing in it, but the strongest man can't hold it much more than a minute.

Answer

Breath

Riddle 40

What room do ghosts avoid?

Answer

The living room.

Riddle 41

*What belongs to you,
but other people use it more?*

Answer

Your name

Riddle 42

What happens once in a lifetime,
twice in a moment,
but never in one hundred years?

Answer
The letter "M"

Riddle 43

What becomes wetter the more it dries?

Answer

Towel

Riddle 44

What comes once in a minute,
twice in a moment,
but never in a thousand years?

Answer

The letter "m".

Riddle 44

What has hands but doesn't clap?

Answer

A clock.

Riddle 45

What belongs to you but is used more by your friends?

Answer

Your name

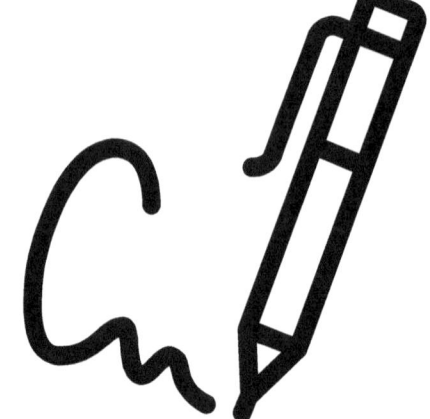

Funny Jokes for Kids

1. Why did the tomato blush?
Because it saw the salad dressing.

2. Why didn't the duck pay for the lip balm?
He wanted to put it on his bill.

3. What do you call an alligator in a vest?
An investigator!

4. Why did Darth Vader turn off one light?
He prefers it on the dark side.

5. What do you call a fly without wings?
A walk.

6. How do you throw a party on Mars?
You planet.

7. Do you have holes in your underwear?
No?
So how do you put your legs through?

8. When is it time to go to the dentist?
Tooth hurty (2:30)

9 What did the frog order at McDonald's?
French flies and Diet Croak.

10. Did you hear about the two guys who stole a calendar?
They both got 6 months.

11. Why didn't the teddy bear eat dessert?
Because he was stuffed.

12. How do you make a tissue dance?
Put a little boogie in it.

13. How did Darth Vader know what Luke Skywalker got him for his birthday?
He felt his presents.

Q: How do all the oceans say hello to each other?
They wave!

Q: What did one wall say to the other wall?
I'll meet you at the corner!

Q: What do you call a bear with no teeth?
A gummy bear!

Q: What do you call cheese that isn't yours?
Nacho cheese!

Q: Where do cows go for entertainment?
To the moo-vies!

Knock, knock. Who's there? Cows go. Cows go who?
No, cows go MOO!

Q: What do you call a cow with no legs?
Ground beef!

Q: What do you call a cow with two legs?
Lean meat!

Q: What do you call a pig that knows karate?
A pork chop!

Q: Why are ghosts bad liars?
Because you can see right through them!

Q: What animal needs to wear a wig?
A bald eagle!

Q: What do you call a fly without wings?
A walk!

Knock knock. Who's there?
A little old lady? A little old lady who?
I didn't know you could yodel!

Q: Why do bees have sticky hair?
Because they use honey combs!

www.ingramcontent.com/pod-product-compliance
Lightning Source LLC
LaVergne TN
LVHW060337080526
838202LV00053B/4490